PERCUSSION ACCOMPANIMENT

MOVIE FAVORITES

Solos and String Orchestra Arrangements
Correlated with Essential Elements String Method

Arranged by
ELLIOT DEL BORGO

Welcome to Essential Elements Movie Favorites! This book is designed to be used as a complement to the STRING ORCHESTRA arrangements. These easy percussion parts may be played by members of the string orchestra or by adding one or two percussion students.

Page #	Title
2	Chariots Of Fire
3	Forrest Gump-Main Title
4	Apollo 13 (End Credits)
5	The John Dunbar Theme
6	Theme From E.T. (The Extra-Terrestrial)
7	Theme From "Jurassic Park"
8	The Man From Snowy River
9	Mission: Impossible Theme
10	Raiders March
11	Somewhere Out There
12	Star Trek® The Motion Picture

ISBN 978-0-7935-8951-7

HAL•LEONARD®
CORPORATION

7777 W. BLUEMOUND RD. P.O. BOX 13819 MILWAUKEE, WI 53213

00868031

T0044795

From CHARIOTS OF FIRE

CHARIOTS OF FIRE

PERCUSSION
Snare Drum, Sus. Cym.

Music by VANGELIS
Arranged by ELLIOT DEL BORGO

00868031

FORREST GUMP-MAIN TITLE

(Feather Theme)

PERCUSSION
Small Shaker, Opt. Small Wood Block, Sus. Cym.

Music by ALAN SILVESTRI
Arranged by ELLIOT DEL BORGO

00868031

From APOLLO 13
APOLLO 13
(End Credits)

By JAMES HORNER
Arranged by ELLIOT DEL BORGO

PERCUSSION *
Snare Drum, Bass Drum,
Sus. Cym., Tambourine

* May be played by one player on drum set.

00868031

THE JOHN DUNBAR THEME

PERCUSSION

Triangle, Wind Chimes,
Wood Blocks, Timpani, Sus. Cym.

By JOHN BARRY
Arranged by ELLIOT DEL BORGO

00868031

From the Universal Picture E.T. (THE EXTRA-TERRESTRIAL)

THEME FROM E.T.

(The Extra-Terrestrial)

PERCUSSION
Wind Chimes, Timpani, Sus. Cym., S.D.

Music by JOHN WILLIAMS
Arranged by ELLIOT DEL BORGO

00868031

From the Universal Motion Picture JURASSIC PARK

THEME FROM "JURASSIC PARK"

PERCUSSION
Triangle, Sus. Cym., Wind Chimes

Composed by JOHN WILLIAMS
Arranged by ELLIOT DEL BORGO

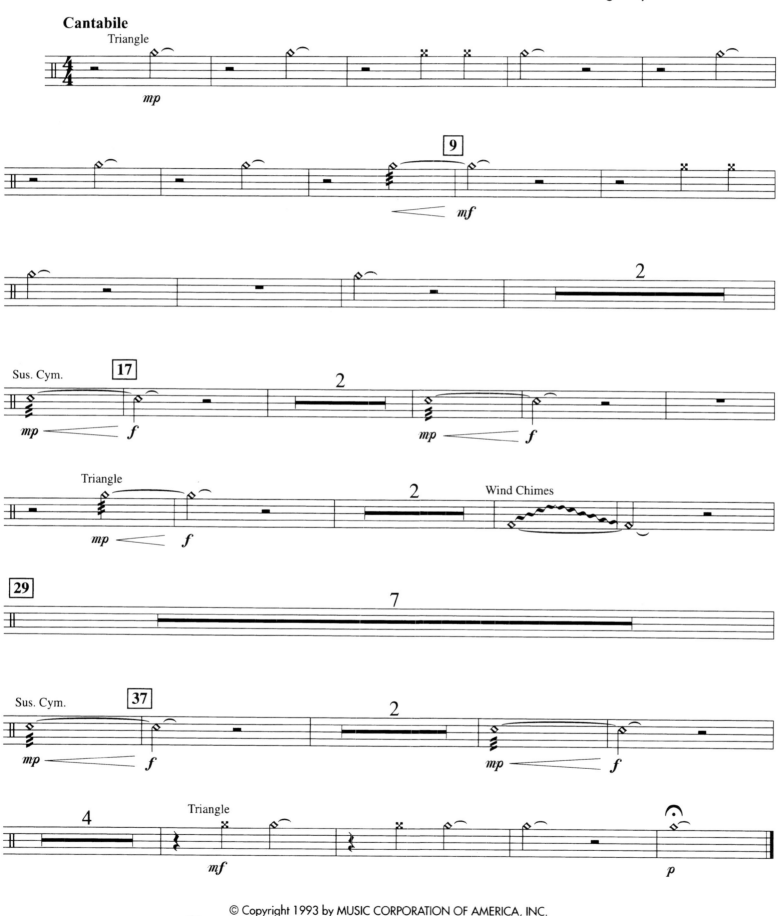

00868031

MCA MUSIC PUBLISHING

THE MAN FROM SNOWY RIVER
(Main Title Theme)

By BRUCE ROWLAND
Arranged by ELLIOT DEL BORGO

PERCUSSION
Wind Chimes, S.D., Tamb., Sus. Cym.

00868031

MISSION: IMPOSSIBLE THEME

By LALO SCHIFRIN
Arranged by ELLIOT DEL BORGO

PERCUSSION
Bongos, Sus. Cym.

Intense
Bongos (with sticks)

00868031

From the Paramount Motion Picture RAIDERS OF THE LOST ARK

RAIDERS MARCH

PERCUSSION *

Snare Drum, Bass Drum, Sus. Cym.

Music by JOHN WILLIAMS
Arranged by ELLIOT DEL BORGO

* May be played by one player on drum set.

00868031

SOMEWHERE OUT THERE

PERCUSSION

Mark Tree, Triangle,
Wind Chimes, Cabasa, Claves

**Words and Music by JAMES HORNER,
BARRY MANN and CYNTHIA WEIL**
Arranged by ELLIOT DEL BORGO

MCA MUSIC PUBLISHING

00868031

STAR TREK® THE MOTION PICTURE

PERCUSSION *
Snare Drum, Bass Drum, Sus. Cym.

Music by JERRY GOLDSMITH
Arranged by ELLIOT DEL BORGO

* May be played by one player on drum set.